T0114648

Also by author:

*When Spirits Speak: Messages
From Spirit Children (2011)*

*When Spirits Speak: A Gathering of Heroes
Stories of U.S. Soldiers in Vietnam (2012)*

When Spirits Speak:
Stiltbird's Last Supper

A Frequency Interrupted -
A New Beginning

JERI K. TORY CONKLIN

Writer

BALBOA.PRESS

A DIVISION OF HAY HOUSE

Balboa Press books may be ordered through booksellers or by contacting:

Balboa Press
A Division of Hay House
1663 Liberty Drive
Bloomington, IN 47403
www.balboapress.com
844-682-1282

Cover Illustration by Teri Ann "Sunny" Henderson
Logo by Chris Addington
Foreword © Reese Maskwa, 2022

Print information available on the last page.

ISBN: 979-8-7652-3043-5 (sc)
ISBN: 979-8-7652-3044-2 (e)

Balboa Press rev. date: 07/15/2022

Dedication

This book is dedicated to all the seekers and dreamers who came into this lifetime knowing who they are and their purpose for making a difference. For those who have "forgotten" who they are/were and the purpose they chose, find your village; it is there waiting—you just have to look. We are never forgotten; our souls know the direction of "home."

Contents

FOREWORD

When we tune in and listen to the spirit world, we tune into lessons that simply cannot be learned in the physical world. Sometimes, it takes death and torture to help others heal and learn the lessons they are meant to learn. There are so many lessons we come to learn and so many lessons we help others learn so we can all grow and evolve. Spirit reminds us that death is only a transition—a transition to the next part of our lives. Spirit also reminds us that our short amount of time here on earth needs not be taken so seriously. We have reincarnated before; we have all done really amazing things, we have all done horrible things, but those horrible things do not need to define our souls.

In my years of being a trauma and spiritual transformational expert, I have learned that it doesn't matter who or what you were in a past life. That will not define who you are at soul level, or who you will be in your next life, should you choose to reincarnate again. It is only we who hold onto the terrible things we do; it is only we who choose to go through these horrendous life lessons. We can, at any time, stop, redirect our lives, and change; it only takes a moment to say, "I will stop this cycle and become who I want to be, in this life and in my future soul's journey." We are all powerful creators; we can create hell in our lives or we can create heaven. That choice is always up to us.

In this book, Jeri does a wonderful job sharing how sometimes, through the bad things we do in life, we can find peace and love again. She encourages us to know that even after death, we still live on and our terrible things can be left in that life. We do not need to carry burdens like revenge into our spirit realm or into future lives. Jeri's line of communication to the spirit world is truly an amazing gift, for I believe her words will change the world and how we see the spirit world. The spirit world is always around us, like Jeri shows us.

Reese Maskwa, a Trauma and Spiritual
Transformational Expert

PREFACE

COMMUNICATING WITH THE SPIRIT WORLD

All beings, whether seen or unseen,
have the ability to communicate with
and understand each other.

I have been communicating with the Spirit World since I was born. I never questioned my ability to speak with or see spirits: those children, adults, or animals whose life energy had left their bodies and moved to the nonphysical plane, or "the other side." I just did not understand why adults did not see or hear them. Then, when I was ten, my Dad was killed, and I shut down my communication with the Spirit World.

In 1994, as an adult, I began to allow spirit communication back into my life when I connected with two earthbound spirit children at my home in Idaho. However, it was not until one day in 2007, as I sat on a beach in Cape Cod, counting the waves, seeking change, and healing, that I realized communicating with the Spirit World and sharing those messages with others must be a way back to living the life I was meant to live. So I listened.

Each and every one of us, not just me, came into this lifetime knowing that we could communicate with the Spirit World. When we are young children, the veil between the spirit home we have just left and our new, earthly home is thin. Not only do we communicate with those spirits we have left behind, but our soul also moves freely between the two dimensions. If we are born into a family that accepts our ability to communicate telepathically with spirits, then we are encouraged and supported. If not, then we bow to social and parental pressures, wrapping our knowledge in oilskin and tucking it away in our secret box where it will be safe until we can use it again.

The means by which I communicate with spirits probably most resembles what we think of as telepathy, or the exchange of information through thought. Telepathic communication has been going on in various cultures since the beginning of time as we know it. Considered a universal ability, telepathy is shared by all as inhabitants of Mother Earth. Before there was a vocal spoken language, telepathic communication—or "mind talk," as I call it—was all there was.

I communicate with the Spirit World using the three most common forms of spiritual communication:

Clairvoyance (visual communication), which allows us to see others' thoughts or information not necessarily with our physical eyes, but rather as colors, forms, and textures in our mind's eye (also known as the third eye). For example, I see entities or spirits as if they were fully embodied people standing right in front of me.

Clairaudience (auditory communication), which allows us to hear others' thoughts or receive information not with our physical ears, but as Voices in our minds. When I speak with spirits, I hear what they are saying as clearly as I hear people in ordinary reality speaking. The Voices of the spirits I hear sound just like those of people I speak with in regular conversations, but I hear their voices within my head.

Clairsentience (tactile communication), in which we pick up thoughts and information and convert them into a feeling, be it emotional or physical. You may feel the information as calming feelings, as a prickly sensation, or as the hairs on your arms and back of your neck standing up. As you begin to differentiate types of spiritual energies, you will come to recognize the different feelings or sensations each triggers for you. For example, when I am in the presence of a spiritual entity, my legs begin to tingle. I can also tell whether an entity has actually left a physical body and is now on the other side, or is still inhabiting a body on the physical plane and using the Spirit World as a means to communicate with me, by how heavy or dense its energy feels.

The spirits that "come through" the spiritual world to me may be those who have left their physical bodies and now are back home in the Spirit World. They may still be inhabiting physical bodies here on earth, known as "earthbound" spirits, who have left their bodies temporarily to meet me on the nonphysical, spiritual plane.

When I telepathically talk with the spirits that come to me, I can only describe my consciousness as a deep meditative state. While my physical body remains in the chair on the physical plane, my soul is in the nonphysical realm, acting as an observer and participant. There I am able to interact with spirits as if we both were still in physical bodies. I see/visualize each spirit as an image with a face and a body. I see its essence and its aura (energy field). Linear time passes while I am away from the physical realm, though I am unaware of its passing. Depending upon how much time I have spent away from my physical body, it can take some time for me to readjust to it when I return.

Communication with the Spirit World can be done at any time, in any place. It does not require anything other than for you to show up and ask questions with respect and appreciation. Communicating with spiritual beings—whether they are angels, fairies, the spirits of children or soldiers who have died, or the spirits of animals, rocks, or trees, those from the star systems, even an executed person—is as simple as sitting quietly and allowing yourself to hear or see what they would have you know. Their Voices are, quite simply the still, small Voice you hear in your head, see in your mind's eye, or feel with your body or emotions.

My work with the Spirit World is inspired by a higher power, which I know as God. Bringing forth spirit stories in a published format is my way of saying, "I am a communicator with the Spirit World—I am known as 'Writer,'" the name given to me by the children who first came through. This is who I am, and what I do. As our souls move into greater spiritual evolution, I believe it is important to see more accounts of communication with the Spirit World in written form, so that others might realize this communication is possible.

I believe that God speaks to and through each of us in many different ways—including through the

Voices of those in the Spirit World—in an attempt to remind us of the home we left behind when our souls chose to incarnate into physical bodies in this lifetime. If you have lost a loved one, please know that person is safe and with God and you can speak with him or her anytime you want.

It is not always easy, or even possible, to document and validate the authenticity of the information provided by those speaking from the Spirit World. Growing in trust and faith in the unseen world is, however, a rewarding experience. With each communication I receive from those who have passed and are in the Spirit World, my faith in my ability to bring forth the gifts they entrust to me grows.

INTRODUCTION

A hush fell over the crowd as the soldiers stood snapping to attention. A pilot walked down the aisle. I knew he was a pilot by the flight suit, the instrument board strapped to his leg, his helmet, and air mask. I knew he was a pilot because he was my dad. With him walked the White Soldier, a spirit who appears on the battlefield to bring soldiers who had passed home.

"No one passes alone," Dad said. "No one passes alone."

Why had he come and brought the White Soldier? Who was going to pass? My eyes scanned the crowd of men and children, seeking who might be coming through next. Jeffery C., the soldier who had come through with the children to ask me to write my last book *When Spirits Speak: A Gathering of Heroes*, stood and came towards me.

"This is for you, Writer," he said, unfolding his hand to present me with a roughly carved small wooden bird with long legs. "It's a stiltbird, Writer.

This is the carver," he said as a tall man moved out from behind him. "The legal system failed him, Writer. Set them straight."

"John Adam Buck. Please call me Johnny," the man said, extending his hand to me. "I guess you will be writing about my last supper and how I got there."

"Glad to meet you Johnny."

As I was waiting for the children and the soldiers to leave, as was customary once they had come to bring me my next "assignment," all eyes turned towards me. My dad stepped forward this time, standing in front of me. "And you, Writer, this is your time as well. We have helped you to find your Voice once again. Use it now. What would your last meal be? A last meal to celebrate/commemorate your life? Perhaps a last meal celebrating the passing of your old life to make way for your new beginnings? Whatever you choose, your new way of life awaits you. Embrace the joy and move forward, sharing your words for all to hear. Many are called, few are chosen, but you are one of the chosen. Allow the words to flow forth and touch us all as we move into new futures, the old ways left behind."

I felt humbled. It was time to go. I had met the person whose story I would tell in this book you are holding, and learned about telling my own story from my dad. Coming to attention, I said, "Thank you for your service" to the soldiers and all who stood before me, raising my right hand in salute for one last time as I watched my dad turn to leave. "I love you Dad," I said. Pausing mid-step, he turned, giving me that smile I knew so well and had missed for all these years. The children quickly ran to embrace me as tears rolled down my cheeks. "I love you Dad."

I am known as Writer to many in the Spirit World, and I write their stories as they tell them to me. This time, I was telling Johnny's story not only from his and the other Voices, but also through information contained in the numerous court documents on file in the Georgia case I believe was his.

I am intrigued by Johnny's story on many different levels. First is because it was so different from what I would normally write. Second, it made me rethink the equality and fairness of our legal system (I was a paralegal for twenty-five years). Third is because of the emotions stirred up by the picking of my symbolic "last meal." I also considered the importance of the role soul groups play throughout our many different lifetimes to help the evolution of our souls, and how my own life was changing. My own last supper choices were the foods I chose in order to leave my old life, my past, behind. My new life was beginning as I came into my own. Throughout this process, I have learned who I really was, who I was meant to be, and what I was meant to do. I relearned my soul's purpose. Now was the time to step forward and take my place amongst the future happenings.

After reading the court documents associated with his case, I knew Johnny was innocent of the killings of Maven and her two daughters. I also knew that there was nothing I could do to change the outcome of Johnny's fate, as that had already been taken care of by his execution/murder.

There were so many different lessons to be learned, even lessons for the many different people involved in the trial process. These people, who all came together to assist Johnny in this physical lifetime, were part of his life plan from the beginning.

I wrote Johnny's story and titled it *Stiltbird's Last Supper* because of the small stiltbird he carved with his grandpappy, and the role it played in my own life. I am not comfortable writing about criminal violence, and I do not enjoy reading about it. Nevertheless, I wrote Johnny's story knowing that, along the way, the message and lessons of the story would appear when they too were ready to be born, just as the stiltbird had risen for Johnny.

While researching Johnny's story, I was drawn to the last meals of other prisoners scheduled for execution. I am an archaeologist and researcher by heart, loving to dig into the *why* and *wherefore* of any number of things. I learned that

> The tradition of the last meal dates back
> to ancient Greece then spreads to Rome,
> where gladiators partook in a final spread
> before entering the coliseum to see out

their punishment. It was then considered a celebration of life before undoubtedly heading into certain death. In the years between then and now, hundreds of different traditions precede the end of life, including a last meal and drink request.[1]

Seated in my writing room, I began searching the web for other last suppers of executed prisoners. I came upon one website that listed executed prisoners and their last meal requests, dating back several years.[2] It was there I was drawn to the name and last meal of a Georgia prisoner executed in 2007.

I am not sure what it was that drew me to this particular prisoner or his last supper, but I knew it was Johnny's story as he had relayed to me early on. I immediately began to research his story further. His meal was very simple, and I started thinking about why he might have chosen those particular foods or dishes. Did they remind him of home? Were they his favorite foods as a child? Why would he choose such simple foods, when he could have had anything he wanted for his last supper? Why choose comfort

---

[1] Nicole Madison, "What are the Restriction[s] on Last Meal[s]?" My Law Questions, last modified June 26, 2022, https://www.mylawquestions.com/what-are-the-restrictions-placed-on-a-last-meal.htm.

[2] This website is no longer operational as of 2013.

foods when you could have expensive gourmet foods such as steak, lobster, or caviar?

As I delved deeper into last suppers, crimes committed, and all the variables that go with same, I searched for patterns, and found none that jumped out. Severity of crime did not correlate with food choices. Race did not seem to have any similarities either. The closest I came to finding any correlation was in the choice of regional foods. Maybe that was solely because of the availability of the foods in that area. Perhaps those last supper food choices were made by the prisoner for whatever memory they would offer him or her at the time of execution. It was one last opportunity to reflect back on the good parts of his or her life.

It only took me a few weeks of reading the court documents on one particular Georgia prisoner to begin to see the similarities between my stiltbird story and the crime he had committed. Somehow, I had found Johnny's actual case and Johnny himself confirmed it.

At least it was my intention to tell you Johnny's story, and up until today I was still on that track moving forward. Then, just as before, my frequency was interrupted. I both heard and felt a Voice tell me this book was, in the end, really about my last supper, the passing of my old ways into the new ways of my future. It was about celebrating a life lived, but honoring and welcoming a new life going forward.

I have put this book together a little differently than a normal novel would read. Any recipes provided are at the end of this book. Please enjoy them. I hope you find them inspiring, and perhaps find your own meanings in them.

Part 1 is called *Stiltbird's Last Supper.* Johnny's story is broken down into chapters under the headings of his last food choices. I have woven them into what was happening to Johnny at that time in his life as he communicated it to me. For some of the food choices, I have provided recipes because I was guided to do so. Johnny loved recounting how his grandmammy would prepare the foods that he had chosen in his growin' up years.

And so it is that I give you Johnny's story, communicated by himself from the Spirit World. Johnny speaks with a deep Southern drawl. Attempting to get the pronunciation and spelling of those words down in their correct spelling form has been difficult. To make the flow of reading Johnny's words easier on all of us, I have used the dropped *g* and the added *s* for some of the plural forms of pronouns. At times, he speaks without the Southern accent, and I have left his account as I heard it.

The story begins with the evening news report of Lizbeth Cort. A little backwards perhaps, but it will help you to understand Johnny's beginning and end and the life he lived in between.

Part 2 is called "Frequency Interrupted." Having researched last meals of Johnny and others who have been executed, I thought of myself. What would my choices be for my last meal? Would I chose comfort foods I had grown up with and the memories I associated with them, or would I choose gourmet foods because I could? I have included the food choices I would make and why to honor my past and let it go. I found myself telling my own story with my Voice and my own words.

Part 3 is called "New Beginnings." Soon after ending parts 1 and 2, Johnny came through and asked me about honoring my future. I had not thought of that, but it made sense. I was letting the past go and, like the phoenix who rises from the flames of the fire, I too had survived the fire and the drought. I was looking forward to my future. What would I choose?

What would you, the reader, choose? Pretend you know it is to be your last day on Earth with your family, heavenly family included. Friends are gathered around and they have each brought you your last food choices to enjoy. What would those food choices be and why?

But what if it weren't your last day. What if, like me, it was a way to honor your past and the memories associated with it, while at the same time, a way to celebrate your new beginnings as you embrace a new you and a new day? What will you chose?

I would love to hear from you about your food choices and why you chose them. Please email me at <u>whenspiritsspeak@yahoo.com.</u>

PROLOGUE
Reporter

...at 12:00 o'clock midnight John Adam Buck will be executed by lethal injection for the felony murders of Maven Watson and her two daughters Edna and Irma. Johnny received his last meal of four fried pork chops, collard greens and boiled okra, white beans and ham hocks, fried corn, fried green tomatoes, cornbread, lemonade, strawberry ice cream, and three glazed donuts. Lizbeth Cort reporting for WAGA Evening News, Atlanta, Georgia.

"That was a tough one," I said tapping my notes on the news desk.

"Don't take it personally," Bob, my cameraman, countered. "You are always so serious when it comes to an execution announcement."

"What if he is innocent? What if he really didn't commit these murders? I've followed this case from the beginning and something just isn't right. Something is missing. While a jury of the Georgia court of law has found him guilty based on circumstantial evidence, I am not convinced that he is in fact guilty of the actual murders of Maven and her two daughters."

"Sometimes the system doesn't work. Sometimes life isn't fair. If he is innocent, even though he has claimed all along that he did in fact commit the murders, then for him, it is just another one of those shitty days." Chuckling at his own joke, Bob turned out the lights to the news studio as we walked out.

A bitter, cold wind was blowing and an earlier dusting of snow covered the ground. Grabbing hold of Bob's elbow, I walked with him to our cars in an effort not to slip on the icy sidewalk.

"Thank you for the wing," I said, unlocking my car.

"You're welcome," said Bob, laughing his characteristic chuckle. "If it bothers you so much, why don't you go on over and watch the execution?"

Would I even want to do that, I asked myself. There was still six hours to go, and I had plenty of time to get there. My investigative news reporter credentials would get me inside, but could/would I morally watch as another human being is put to sleep, much like the family pet after years of unconditional love and faithful service? Is it not euthanasia by another definition, and isn't that illegal in the human sector of our society?

The wind buffeted my car, rocking it side to side. An omen perhaps of the proverbial rocking my own moral boat? Calling the station manager for permission, I started my car and drove towards the Georgia State Prison in Reidsville. Not only was my moral boat being rocked, but also my interest had been piqued by Johnny's last meal request. Why would he choose the meal he chose? Was there a cultural significance, or was it just comfort food?

Blowing snow brought my attention back to the road ahead. Only four more miles to go and yet, for John Adam Buck, it was the end of his road. Would he know that it was a bitter cold, snowy night outside? Would he know that for this moment, at least one person thought/knew he was innocent and the system had failed him by not introducing important evidence that would clear him? The lights of Georgia State Prison loomed in front of me. Such a beautiful building; such a horrendous act to be taking place. Showing my reporter's pass to the security guard, I was directed to the parking lot and escorted inside.

INSIDE THE DEATH CHAMBER

News reporters are supposedly unbiased witnesses. There was nothing unbiased about me. I knew they were executing an innocent man, yet there was nothing I could do. All the news reporters were seated together in a waiting room of sorts. As my name was called, I lined up and left the waiting room to take my place in the viewing room behind the glass that housed the death chamber.

We were seated in the back of the room. In the front row sat those who had come on behalf of the condemned. There was only one person seated on Johnny's side—a fifty-ish looking woman. I would later learn her name was Holly. The other chairs were filled with those involved in Johnny's arrest and prosecution. The only one there for the Watson family was a man named Thaddeus, Maven's husband and father of the two girls.

At the moment, the curtain allowing viewing access to the death chamber was closed.

When the curtain was opened, Johnny was alone, strapped on a gurney in the execution chamber, a small room with white cinderblock walls. I was able to see him through the glass window. A sheet covered his body. A tube in his arm was threaded through a hole in the wall where the medical doctor stood, ready to administer a lethal cocktail. Johnny lay motionless, staring at the ceiling as Warden Jones read the execution order signed by Chatham County Judge Hazelton. Warden Jones then asked Johnny if he had any last words.

Johnny turned his head, looked at Thaddeus, smiled, and said, "The Stiltbird has had his last supper and he's ready to fly away now."

I saw Johnny's eyes scan the room, stopping on Holly. I noticed Holly raise her hand to her heart and then, bringing the fingers of her right hand to her lips, she blew Johnny a last kiss. His eyes twinkled and he smiled in acknowledgment of her kindness.

Just as the first of three drugs that would end Johnny's life were being injected, Thaddeus jumped up and banged on the window separating him from Johnny. Reaching into his coat pocket, he pulled out the carved stiltbird, showing it to Johnny.

"He's innocent. I killed my wife and daughters. I killed them," Thaddeus shouted, "not my son."

I didn't know what would happen next, but I was sure glad I'd driven up to Reidsville tonight. A story was about to break, and I was going to break it.

Guards rushed in, and pretty much pandemonium ensued. The last thing I saw as I was being pushed out with everyone else was the doctor injecting the last syringe with its lethal cocktail into Johnny's arm.

The lights did not go out in Georgia State Prison that night as lawyers scrambled, cops drew weapons, people began running.

I slipped through the mass of bodies and headed down the long hallway maze out into the freezing night air. Taking a deep breath, I exhaled into the night. *Breathe,* I kept telling myself, *breathe.* Slip sliding my way across the icy sidewalks to the skating rink parking lot, I found my car covered in a fresh layer of snow. I quickly got inside, started the engine, and turned on the heater. I wanted to sit and digest all of what had just happened, to write it down before the order of events got lost. Instead, I drove out of the parking lot as fast as I dared. I would stop somewhere between here and home to record the events. I knew I wouldn't get any sleep tonight.

Going into my office the next morning, I was greeted by Bob.

"Heard you had quite a night in Reidsville."

"That's an understatement," I said. "You won't believe the story I have to tell. We have some work to do."

> ...at 11:58 o'clock midnight John Adam Buck was murdered by lethal injection for three crimes he did not commit. Thaddeus Watson was arrested for the felony murders of his wife Maven Watson and their two daughters Edna and Irma. Lizbeth Cort reporting for WAGA evening News, Atlanta, Georgia.

Part 1

Stiltbird's Last Supper

"Sandpiper" is the name given for a large family of small shore birds. Sandpipers have long legs and slender bills for probing in the wet sand for their prey. As wading birds they feed on all sorts of small invertebrates. Their coloring is dull with brown or gray above and buff with streaks of spots below. A relative of the common sandpiper is the "Stilt Sandpiper" distinguished from its cousins by its much longer and paler legs.

Told to me by Johnny as he reflected back on his lifetime. I am writing it from his perspective.

To take a raw chunk of wood out of a swamp and turn it into a beautiful wood carvin' with a number of different saws and knives was a skill I learned as a young man. As I sat watchin' the house for shadowed movement, I thought back to the many long hours I spent at my grandpappy's knees in piles of fragrant wood shavin's. Them's were the good years, and little did I know them's would end as fast as them's had begun.

Grandpappy had painstakin'ly showed me how to hold a chunk of wood in my small hands and feel for the image to emerge. At first it seemed to take forever, and I grew impatient after havin' spent many days continuin' to hold the wood waitin'. Waitin' to see an image appear. While I was short on patience, I was long on vision. I knew I would see it appear. For I had dreams—dreams I didn't tell a soul about.

Not all my dreams were happy. I saw in my future, not-too-distant future, I was by myself, lost in the maze of a cornfield. Grandpappy always told me, "If you's get lost, can't find your grandmammy or me, you's just sit down and wait, we's'll come find you's; we's always will."

But in the dream no one ever came for me. I didn't like this dream and woke up shoutin' for my grandpappy or grandmammy. Other times I would see myself at the ocean's edge, watchin' the stiltbirds scurry ashore as each wave rolled in. I liked this dream better. It gave me hope on many different levels. One, that I would one day be a grown-up man at the seashore, and two, that a stiltbird was comin' to my block of wood.

While I waited for my image to appear, Grandpappy told me stories of his own trip to the ocean as a young boy.

"My own father took me to the shore once. It was so long ago that many of the details have faded from my mind, but what does remain are the memories of the stiltbirds, as I called them. Small-bodied birds on long, thin legs, scurryin' back and forth in the foam each time the waves roll in and out. Their long slightly curved bills probin' the wet sand for their next meal. I was entertained for hours by these busy birds. As the waves rolled in the flock would scurry as one out of its way only to return as one to poke in the sand as it receded. Up and down, up and down."

Grandpappy's eyes were closed now, perhaps he was back at the shore rememberin' that time long ago. I let him sleep.

A few days later as I sat waitin', I thought of my grandmammy and the hours she spent on her knees prayin' to someone she called *God* who lived in the sky. And so, on bended knees in the middle of Grandpappy's wood shavin's, I prayed to that man in the sky for an image to appear. Grandmammy says, "God listens all too well to the prayers of young children." Soon thereafter, a very basic and simple image of a sea bird took hold in the piece of wood with its small round body with pencil-thin legs that looked like *stilts*. In my mind, I saw the stiltbird of my grandpappy's stories and my own visions emerge and scurry across the sand, weavin' to miss the foamy waves as they's rolled to shore.

"Gramps, it's here!" I cried, clutchin' my wood as if it were a piece of gold and runnin' on my own skinny legs to where Gramps stood under the willow tree. "Do you's see it?" I asked breathlessly, handin' the wood over to my grandpappy's knobby hands. "It's a bird on stilts," I crowed at the top of my lungs. "Do you's see it?" my excitement overflowin'.

"Yes, Son, I do," said Gramps. "It's a beautiful bird, meant just for you's. Shall we's go and draw it out so you's can start carvin'?" My small hand tucked inside of his large hand, we's walked back to the woodshop. A bird on stilts was about to be born.

WHITE BEANS AND HAM HOCKS, COLLARD GREENS, AND BOILED OKRA

No one can say for sure why evil happens, though many have written volumes on the subject. My grandpappy was a harmless man. He and Grandmammy would never hurt anyone; in fact, they's would have shared all they's had with someone down on their luck. That's how Grandpappy saw those down on their luck, just someone down on their luck, needin' a helpin' hand.

"It happens to all of us at least once in our life," Grandpappy said. "Never fail to reach out and extend a helpin' hand to those in need. It will give you's a good feelin', Son."

The garden exploded with the fruits of our hard labor as summer crept toward fall. Grandpappy left me holdin' a new piece of wood, havin' finished my bird on stilts. Grandmammy called for my help bringin' in the vegetable baskets full of collard greens, okra, corn, and several baskets full of tomatoes. I knew what to expect when it was harvest time: my favorite dinner of collard greens, boiled okra, white beans, ham hocks, and cornbread. I could already taste it as my mouth began to water. We's ate simple on the farm, and by most standards we's ate well. Many a-night strangers sat at our table and shared from the farm's surplus. There is much to learn from

5

those who share your meal. Tonight Grandmammy made fried corn—a treat we's only got on special occasions.

The table was set with an extra plate as always. On nights when no one stopped by, Grandmammy said, "It was the Lord's seat, and He was a-joinin' us." Just as we's raised our heads from sayin' our blessin's, there was a soft knock on the screen door.

"Come on in," Grandpappy called. "There's plenty here to share."

"Thank you," the stranger said, leanin' his carryin' pole by the door. "Don't mind if I do. I'm a mite hungry; been walkin' since sunrise."

Drifters all shared one thing in common I noticed—they's was dreamers. There was nothin' tyin' them to the moment or the place. Some carried their possessions in handkerchiefs tied to poles as if they's was goin' off for a day of fishin' at the nearest creek. Others carried cardboard suitcases strapped together with bits and pieces of leather or twine. All was just dreamers passin' through, passersby on a long journey to who knew where. One day I would join them, for I had promised myself I, too, would see the world beyond the borders of the farm. I would see the seashore and the stiltbirds Grandpappy had seen.

I asked him, "Where's you's headed?"

Puttin' down his fork, the stranger got a dreamy look on his face and said, "To the ocean. I've always wanted to see the ocean. My pappy was a seafarin' man and told us stories of fish this big," he said, spreading his hands wide. "I just want to see for myself. My pappy says there is quietness you find sailing on her waters all day long. I want to find that peace for me. I am tired of always running, always looking behinds me. I just want to stop running."

I's showed the dreamer my carvin' of the stiltbird and told him how it was born from my grandpappy's own stories.

Grandmammy reached out and patted his sun-tanned arm. "You's'll find what you's lookin' for," she said as a big smile crossed her face. It was obvious she had a direct line of communication to the man in the sky; perhaps she knew this dreamer's fate. Did she know her own or Grandpappy's on this night?

FRIED CORN

The stranger, havin' filled his stomach and fed my dreams with tales of his many adventures along the road, gathered his carryin' pole and said his goodbyes to us. Sittin' on the porch, we's watched as he walked off down that long country road that would, eventually, lead him to that ocean he was searchin' for.

Grandmammy washed the dishes whilest Grandpappy and I dried. Bein's that I wasn't tall enough to reach the upper cabinets yet, I sat the dishes on the table. Stacked 'em neatly in piles so as to make it easier to put them away later on. Night chores done, Grandpappy and I sat in the porch swing. Grandmammy rocked in her rocker, hummin' "Amazing Grace." I don't know how many verses it really had, but the hummin' went on until the fireflies, havin' danced in the darkened sky, said their own goodnight and settled in the trees. As if a switch had been flipped, all at once the trees went dark.

Grandpappy stood and gently shook Grandmammy's shoulder. "Time to go in, sweetheart," he mumbled. Turnin' off the lights, Grandpappy shut the door behind us as we's headed for bed.

Perhaps I should have known that somethin' was amiss, as I looked out my window, not yet ready for bed. The full moon cast a silvery pathway onto the cornfields. I thought I had seen a movement in the shadows but perhaps not. Perhaps it was just one of the night creatures runnin' through the cornfield on its way to the hunt. Turnin' away from the window I settled in my bed and pulled Grandmammy's handmade quilt up over my head.

The moonlight filtered in castin' shadows on the walls. If only I had been brave enough to pay attention that night perhaps I would have seen the flames dance in silhouettes as they's sprang from the cornfield, creepin' their way toward the house. I didn't though. I didn't hear or smell a thing. Not even Grandpappy and Grandmammy bein' murdered in their bed as they's slept cradled in each other's arms. The sheriff believes that I may have passed the killer comin' out of the house as I pushed my way outside, chokin' on the smoke fillin' the house.

Neighbors were quick to come and help put out the fire, but it wasn't quick enough to save my Grandpappy and Grandmammy. In the beginnin' we's just thought they's had burnt to death. It was much later that I would learn they's had been murdered.

SHORTCAKE AND STRAWBERRIES

I watched the sun come up that next morning. I oftentimes sit and wonder—if'n we's hadn't shared our supper with that stranger; if'n I hadn't turned away from the movement in the cornfield—would any of this happen? Where was that man in the sky Grandmammy prayed to? Where had He been? It wasn't a random murder like they's said; I knew it had been the stranger. He had doubled back and waited until we's was in bed before comin' back in. Grandpappy and Grandmammy didn't have much, nothin' worth stealin' anyways. What was it he was after? With the fire burnin' up all we's had, there was no way to tell what if'n anythin' was missin'.

In all the confusion and with so many things goin' on right now, I just disappeared into the barn and went back to holdin' that piece of wood in my hands.

What was it grandpappy used to say? "If'n you's ever get lost, just sit down where's you's are and we's will come for you's." I was so lost, so I just sat down to wait. Closin' my eyes, I saw his face—the face of the stranger. I knew what I had to do. I worked all day and night a' carvin' that face. Every little nook and cranny, every line and them eyes, they's was the hardest, but I captured them, right down to that dreamin' look.

Gatherin' my simple carvin' tools in an old rag, I found me a branch and tied my pouch to it and started that long walk into town.

"Sheriff," I said tryin' to see above the tall desk. "Sheriff," I said, raisin' my arms and wavin'. "Here's the man that kilt my Grandpappy and Grandmammy," I said handin' the wood carvin' of the stranger's face to the sheriff.

"Johnny, where have you been? We have been looking all over for you."

"In the barn carvin' this for you's. Find him please sheriff. He's a headed for the ocean."

"How do you know that Johnny?"

"He shared dinner with us the night of the fire. Said he was a goin' to the ocean. We's watched him walk off down the road that night. Why Sheriff, why?"

"I wish I knew Johnny. I wish I knew. Now what are we going to do with you?"

That really was the question—what to do with me. I had nowhere to go, no family, lest none I knew about. My mama had dropped me off at my Grandpappy's farm one night and she just never came back.

"Sheriff, I don't have much, just my carvin' tools," I said pointin' to my pouch on the stick. "I'm a mite hungry and all. If'n you's could spare me a nickel or so I'll find a way to pay it back, I promise."

"Johnny let's go over to the café and have some of Anna Mae's shortcakes." That was the best news I had heard in the past few days. "We'll figure out what we are going to do with you after we have a full stomach," he said laughing.

They's never caught the stranger, at least not before I left town several years later.

FRIED GREEN TOMATOES

As the years passed I too became a stranger at many a small town table, sharin' my stories of adventure as I wandered down those dusty, twisted roads. I carried the carved stranger's face with me always askin' if anyone had seen him pass this way. I didn't know what I would do if'n I found him, I just knew that for this moment I was searchin' for him. The question "why" had burned within me over all these years, just like the fire that burned down my home.

Eventually I ended up at the ocean, miles and miles of sand upon which the waves rolled in and out, never stoppin'. It was there I saw the bird on stilts I had first carved as a young boy. Carefully unwrappin' the wooden carvin' I sat it down in the wet sand and backed away. Planted amongst others just like it, would they's accept or reject its likeness? After a few minutes, the stiltbirds no long paid it any attention and began to move in and around it as if it was just one more of their own. How easily it had blended in with its own kind. Perhaps that was the message it was sendin' me— just plant you'srself and you's too will blend in.

Findin' a sand dune to shelter me from the wind, I lay down and slept knowin' I had arrived. Tomorrow I would figure out how to go about findin' the stranger who had murdered my Grandpappy and Grandmammy, for surely he too had arrived at the ocean of his dreams.

TIN CAN CORNBREAD

Cornmeal and water

Tin can cornbread ain't so bad when you's finally figure out the right combination of cornmeal and water. Not as good as that made with lard and eggs, but sometimes you's just experiment. I never complained that my cornbread was a little stiff and didn't melt in my mouth like Grandmammy's used to, but many a stranger who shared my fire did. I just searched their faces for recognition, not seein' the one I was lookin' for. I listened to their stories. On occasion I would pull out my carvin' and ask if'n they's had seen anyone who looked like *him*. No one had and after several months I moved further down the beach to another small town. I sat up a small table I had found partially covered by blowin' sand and I began to carve small trinkets to sell. The ocean washed up plenty of driftwood, sea shells, and sea glass for the takin'. So I began to add the small pieces of sea glass and shells into my creations. The white folks seemed to like what I made and I worked day and night sometimes just to keep my supply up.

HONEY SWEETENED LEMONADE

Honey, water, and lemon juice

There was one fine lady who came by every day to look at what I had made. She was a sight to behold, a liquid sunshine that quenches your thirst on a hot day. Her long blond hair always shinin' and her smile as big as the quarter moon layin' down. She always had kind words to say to me about my work. After a while, I noticed she seemed lost at times, as if the same fog that came in each mornin' with the tide covered her. There was sadness, a deep sadness hidden behind her smile. When there weren't any customers millin' about, she and I talked of the places we's had been and how we's came to be at the ocean. Seems the call to the ocean runs deep in many a dreamer's soul.

Her name was Holly and she had come from a place called New York. I didn't know where it was havin' grown up poor in the south with little book learnin', but it seemed a mighty fine place and one I would like to visit one day. Holly had married and moved here with her husband who was a teacher at the university.

It took quite a few days before her story finally came tumblin' out and with it the pain that clouded her soul. Her husband, havin' grown up in the south, had opened their door to a stranger and shared their meal with him. Later that night he came back to kill them. He had succeeded in killin' her husband James, but only wounded her. She was somehow able to escape the fire and live. But she lived with the memory of that night frozen in time. No wonder she was so sad, I too felt her pain. I knew I too had met this *stranger.*

I didn't immediately put two and two together and connect her *stranger* with my *stranger;* it didn't seem possible as too many years had passed. Then one day I reached in my pack and took out the carvin' and handed it to her.

"Where did you get this?" she screamed.

"I carved it," I said, watchin' the recognition register on her face.

"This is the man who killed my husband and tried to kill me," she said throwing the carving in the sand.

"Are you sure?" I asked. "Because, it is the man who killed my Grandpappy and Grandmammy and then set the field to fire to cover up his tracks."

"Yes, I'm sure," she said, having fallen onto the sand, her hands still shaking. "I will remember that face forever," she said, starting to cry.

I didn't know what to do. Holly and I had shared a terrible memory. One man had destroyed two lives; we's were connected in sadness and loss. I reached over and put my arm around her and pulled her

Jeri K. Tory Conklin

close and together we's cried for those we's had lost and the lives we's might have had but for the *stranger* who had crossed our path in a different place and a different time.

ONE PINT OF STRAWBERRY ICE CREAM

I knew now what I had to do. My carvin's had brought me a fair sum of money tucked away in my sock. After sleepin' on it overnight, I decided it was time to find the *stranger.* He had obviously been here just a few years ago. If I was him, where would I go next? Holly didn't come by that mornin', as she had grown akin to doin'. So I left a small carved heart shaped with sea glass and wood for her on a rock by our spot. I doubted we's would ever meet again, but I wanted her to know that I was goin' to find the *stranger* for both of us. With that, I sat off down the beach for the next small beach community.

Walkin' is good for clearin' your mind and puttin' things in perspective. As I walked I began to plan for when I found the *stranger.* It wasn't that I wouldn't find him; it was just a matter of *when* I would. Patience and vision, that is what grandpappy and carvin' had taught me—patience and vision. Then as luck would have it I saw him. He was older for sure, his hair a little grayer, but I knew it was him.

THREE GLAZED DONUTS

He was with a woman and what appeared to be her two daughters. Not wantin' to be seen just yet, I settled down behind some tall sea grass and watched. The *stranger* appeared to know this woman and her daughters well as they's appeared quite familiar with each other. The younger girl enjoyed wrappin' herself around his legs as he lifted her through the air crabbin' his way down to the wet sand where he would drop her. It was a mad dash by both to reach the dry sand before the next wave rolled in. After a while they's both fell exhausted in the sand and the woman and older daughter joined them. Perhaps he had settled down and gotten himself a family. Just seemed wrong that he could wreak such havoc in the lives of others and still find happiness for himself.

It was a long day as I sat and watched, thinkin' about my plan. First I had to follow them and see where they's lived. The sun rose higher in the sky and the sea grass offered little shade. I soon fell asleep listenin' to their sounds of laughter. The tides turned as the sun fell from the sky. A stem of sea grass bent over in the breeze tickled me awake. I quickly sat up and looked around knowin' I had lost them. "Now what?" I asked myself searchin' in all directions. Rememberin' the lesson of the sandpiper:

"just plant yourself and you's too will blend in," I heard the waves whisper. And so I did. Just as before, I sat up a small table and carved trinkets gifted by the ocean. One thing about murderers, they's don't deviate from their routines much. True to form the *stranger* and his family appeared at the beach a few days later. He seemed more subdued this time. The younger daughter tried to get him to play with her but he shouted for her to go on and play by herself and let him be. He sat alone in the sand with that dreamer's face lookin' out to sea while the woman and her daughters wandered over to my makeshift table. Both girls "ohhed" and "ahhed" pickin' up one babble after another. Finally havin' touched them all, each settled on one small trinket and fished the treasured pennies from their small purses. The older woman looked into my eyes as if she could see through me. Did she know who I was? Could she read my mind and know what I planned to do? I felt as if I knew her and yet, we's had never met, at least not in this lifetime that I remembered.

Walkin' back to her husband sittin' in the sand, she gently touched him on the shoulder, "Thaddeus, it's time to go," she said pointing away from the beach. This time I was ready, and stayin' a safe distance behind, I followed them as they's walked hand in hand up the road and across the street, down two more blocks and finally turned onto their sidewalk. It was a modest house, not in the worst of southern neighborhoods. It looked comfortable and neat. It was obvious that the woman enjoyed gardenin' for she had quite a few flowers addin' vibrant color to an already colorful mix of oleander and camellia bushes. Retracin' my steps back to my beach hideaway I gathered up my carvin's and tools and under cover of night returned to the now quiet house. No one ever seemed to notice me sittin' on the bench at the bus stop corner down from the house, or when I moved across the street and leaned on the lamppost. Just like the wooden bird on stilts, I had just become one of them.

FOUR FRIED PORK CHOPS

I hid outside the home in a circle of oleander bushes just as dusk began to fall. There was no way I could be seen, my body color blendin' with the dark summer foliage. I had been watchin' the house for the past several weeks, learnin' the routines of its occupants, their comin's and goin's noted carefully and methodically in my dime store notebook. Pencil stubs had been cast into the underbrush when the lead no longer provided a function.

> *There was a time when I had been cast off just like the pencil stub I now held. When I could no longer work due to an unfortunate accident, I felt useless. All my life I had struggled to hold down a job. It wasn't that I didn't want to work. I did! I wasn't the lazy type. I took pride in my work and made sure that my product was of quality and that all who bought it would enjoy it for many years to come. And so it came to be that I did the carvin's and made the trinkets out of driftwood, sea shells, and sea glass.*

It wasn't long after that, that I noticed the man leavin' each evening rather early and returnin' early the next morning several times a week. I had followed him on several occasions, only to watch him go into another house, similar to his own. A woman much younger than his wife walked him out in the early hours of the morning and kissed him "goodbye" I suppose. They's were not very discrete and rarely pulled the shade in the bedroom. A small lamp burnin' across the room cast shadows of their bodies movin' in unison and hunger till they's both were spent.

It was time and my plan was in place. I knew his routines well and I waited within the circle of oleander bushes for him to leave. It would definitely happen tonight. Once he had rounded the corner and the lights had gone off in his own home, I grabbed my knife and entered. I knew the layout of the house by heart havin' watched these past few weeks from my hiding place. It didn't take long and not a sound was made. It was quick and clean. I suppose I should have felt somethin' killin' this mother and her daughter, but I didn't. I was fumblin' in my pocket to find a kerchief to wipe the blood off'n my hands when the door burst open. I was still holdin' the carved stiltbird in my hand when the sheriff walked in. I quietly dropped it on the floor unnoticed. Would the stranger find it? Would he remember killin' my grandparents? I would.

A CONVERSATION WITH JOHNNY

W: Writer/J: Johnny

J: You's have written my story well, Writer. You's aren't too far off in what happened. Those missin' years were just that—missin' years. I's went missin' myself. I's was so full of anger at the senseless killin' of my grandparents. They's was good people.

Writer, why am I's here? Why was I's convicted and executed for a crime I's didn't commit?

W: Because society used that last second to kill you. Your own murder was committed by the person giving you the injection. As I understand from the reporter, Lizbeth, when everything started going crazy, Warden Jones held up his hand to stop the injection. The medical doctor, seeing what might be coming, had already started the last of the injections anyway. Phones were flying out, people running to get someone of authority to stop the execution. But it was already too late.

J: I's was a bad man anyway so it don't matter.

W: You weren't a bad man, Johnny. You may have had bad thoughts, but you weren't a bad man. Johnny what you didn't get to hear was Thaddeus saying, "This is my son. He is innocent. I'm the one that killed all of my family." They were all the family you never got to know. Not that it makes it any easier.

J: I's knew killing was wrong. Grandmammy would have been mighty disappointed in me for what I's done. I's even heard her whispering in my ear that night, "Don't do this Johnny boy, don't do this. No good can come from this." Still I's did it, Writer.

I's really just intended to kilt him, not his family. The family done me no wrong. Why did I's go after's his family? It's true he kilt the only family I's knew, but killin' his family would only make it easier for him to move on to his new family. Why would I's want to do that? Why would I's want to help him out like that?

W: Revenge? Justice?

J: Revenge, yes. Justice? Justice for a black man killin' a white man's black family? They's was just happy I's done it. No one was going to work to get me off, why would they? I's was just one more black man off their streets.

You's know, Writer, it alls turned out okay, we's all together here in Heaven. We's a family again. My momma and sisters, I's wish I's got to meet them before. Thaddeus will be comin' soon. Lizbeth told them, Writer, but they's wouldn't listen. She had it all figured out beforehand didn't she. Only she believed in my innocence and I's had no clue.

Part 2

Frequency Interrupted

*Not the end, but the beginning of all that is
new. The old has passed away, the new
is all around us. Breathe it in, allow it to
become part of your soul, part of who you are,
who you strive to be. The new I AM waiting,
waiting for the invitation to be recognized.*

It has been a long seventy-one years to date, as I
begin the process of getting rid of "stuff"—physical,
mental, and emotional—accumulated throughout
all these years. I continue to find pieces of me
everywhere I look. I love finding old notebooks,
journals, tablets of paper, scraps of paper in some
cases. All contain questions I have posed to myself
throughout the years in an attempt to discover who
I really am—my place in this lifetime's picture. Some
of these writings have dates, so I can understand the

timeframe of the questions. Others I can only guess at, being grateful I made it through the experience in most incidences.

I have noticed that there is a pattern scattered throughout when I find a timeline. I pose a question, Spirit gives me an answer, and then I go and screw it up. The lessons are soon forgotten until the next time when I search again.

SOUL GROUPS AND THEIR ROLES
IN OUR LIFETIMES

I became aware of soul groups early on in my education from the Spirit World. Though I did not have such a formal name for them in the beginning, I knew I recognized the players in my current lifetime, knowing we had been together before in other lifetimes.

I have done numerous past-life regressions on myself and others in an effort to identify and understand the role my current family members play in this lifetime. When I read Robert Schwartz's *Your Soul's Plan: Discovering the Real Meaning of the Life You Planned Before You Were Born,* I began to understand the organization and workings of the soul group. In this book, he introduces the concept of pre-birth planning sessions. For a more in-depth understanding, I recommend you read his book. In my book, I will lay it out as I understand it and how it is applicable to my soul group.

Pre-birth sessions are held before each physical lifetime. The different souls decide the roles they will play and the lessons that can be learned by each in such roles. By exchanging roles in the different lifetimes, each soul has a chance to balance out its karma. If, for instance, I murdered you in the last lifetime, you would have the opportunity to murder me in this lifetime. At soul level, this is understood and celebrated for the growth it provides the soul. On a physical level, one feels the pain and emotional connections associated with killing another human being, yet this is where growth comes from.

In Johnny's case, he planned his lifetime and all the players that would participate before he was born. Let me say now rather than later that even with a plan in hand when coming into physical, I believe that said plans can, and oftentimes do, change for one reason or another. That said, I still believe that events will occur to bring about the lesson(s) planned early on. Others from the soul group may step in to fill the spot, or the soul will learn the lesson still by playing a different role, by making a different choice. Any number of last minute unknowns can factor in. I believe at night our souls leave our physical bodies and return to non-physical form to reenergize themselves. Perhaps then is when they make small changes to the plan if need be. All of this soul group information makes complete and total sense to me as I understand it.

My hope is that this book will allow you pause to reflect on all the people who have played a part in your own lifetimes. Did you know you had been with them before? What roles did they play? When did you recognize them from before?

I was my mother's mother in a past life, and she was my daughter. I spent that lifetime pushing her away. She was my daughter and I could not love her, or perhaps I did love her, just not in the way she needed to be loved. Our roles are switched in this lifetime as she is my mother. While I know she loves me, I struggled to be loved by her in the way I need to know I am loved. I have spent this lifetime trying to please my mother in every way possible. Still, I wait to hear those eleven words that will set me free—"I am proud of you in all that you have become." I have spent this lifetime attempting to reconcile with my "self" that I am a good person, whether or not my mother can ever say those words. As the years passed, I realized that time was getting short, and if Alzheimer's or dementia got there first, I might never hear them from her. Will I be okay with that? Why did I so desperately crave that validation from her?

My dad has been my father and my best friend (both male and female roles) in each lifetime we shared. It would take me many years in this lifetime to understand how my dad could leave me when I was ten years old. And then one day, I understood. I am forever grateful to him for allowing me those years to search for an answer to that ever present question: "How can any parent leave his or her child at such a young age?"

My sister has always been a sister in past lifetimes, but has taken on different challenges of sisterhood throughout. In this lifetime, she is the "perfect one," the one who has always done it all the "right way." She was born six years too late for me to follow in her footsteps. I think my role was to make it possible for her to outshine me for the rest of our journey together and I am okay with that.

My brother has been my husband in past lives, always taking on a demanding and domineering role. His disdain of women who try to have a Voice has carried through in this lifetime. I feel his wrath and disrespect, understand where it comes from, and grow my own soul in the process of finding ways to love him now as my brother.

Assembling my final plate, what parts of my past were memorable enough to put onto it? So many events happened that shaped who I was through the years. How would I be able to shift through them all and come up with the most important ones? It was not easy, and I really had no order for the foods I had chosen. I believe in the end, it was the events/ lessons themselves that chose the order.

MILK COFFEE WITH MY DAD

My baby years I spent riding in front of my dad on our horse Honey, as he went about doing cattle chores on South Mountain. I am sure this is where my love of horses came into being. However, it is another memory I will always cherish—those mornings I spent sitting at grandma's dining room table, drinking milk coffee while my Dad drank his coffee and smoked his Camel cigarettes. I could have done without the cigarette smoke, and I am grateful that later on I did not have issues from second-hand smoke. I felt so grown up to be sitting there with Grandma and Dad as they discussed all sorts of topics, most of which were grown-up topics. Occasionally, I would weigh in with my opinion as seen through the eyes of a five year-old. I may not have known much at my young age, but I knew that no matter what, I did not want to out-grow those mornings with my Dad and milk coffee.

Still, I could feel there was something they were not saying. I could feel it intuitively, see it in their facial expressions when they would look my way, speaking in hushed tones. I knew it was about something that happened to me around the age of three. What did they know and were not talking about? What had I done to merit such glances and hushed whispers?

Little did I know that a few short years later, my dad would be killed while flying for the U.S. Navy and I would not see him again in the physical world. All those mornings, all those opportunities to say, "I love you" and tell him how much he meant to me were gone. It is funny, but riding on Honey with my dad and doing cow chores at the barn, fishing off the old rickety pier, and trips to the beach are all I remember about interaction times with my dad. That's not much for ten years of being together.

Any secrets have gone to the grave with those who knew, or have been buried deep in the memory of those still living.

Fifty-two years later, I would remember the "event" in 2013 while working on this book. It just popped in one day. At least I remembered and a handful of puzzle pieces that had not seemed to fit together finally made sense, and took their place in the corner. My inner child had protected me from this "event" for all these many years, and for that I am grateful. I realize now how this event has unconsciously/silently shaped my life through the years, and still I have survived. Perhaps in the end, my dad's passing was his gift to me.

Knowing this secret now passed onto me for safekeeping, I chose to remember the good times with my dad—the early mornings around grandma's table drinking milk coffee with him. To this day, I drink my milk coffee (one-half coffee and one-half milk) with fond memories of mornings with my dad, when the cares of the world were far away, in some other kitchen.

In those last few hours of my life, I would like to return to my grandma's dining room table and have milk coffee with my dad one more time. I would always wonder if there was something I could have said during our morning coffee that would have changed his destiny and kept him around longer to watch me grow up into who I am today. Who other than my dad would he have been today? If I would have known our future, I would have asked him what I should do if something ever happened to him. I would have told him how much I loved him, for I knew nothing different. He was still my dad.

I tried to raise my own daughter on milk coffee and spend our mornings around the dining room table talking about our days and how they would unfold. There was nothing about milk coffee that interested her, and talking with Mom was definitely not hip.

MOM'S FROSTED MEATLOAF

There is nothing better in my world than my mom's meatloaf with its spices and brown sugar frosting. Why? Because I know that the next day, without fail, I will be eating the most delicious cold meatloaf sandwiches, and those sandwiches are what I love best about mom's meatloaf. The spices in the meat have blended together overnight and the frosting is the most flavorful. There is just something about the marriage of the brown sugar and spices that frost the top of the meatloaf and the meatloaf itself that is key to this memory.

Of course, the meatloaf is also delicious that first night and I eat my fill of its warm, rich taste, but I make sure there is always plenty left over for sandwiches the next day. Looking back on my life, I realize some of the choices I have made in many ways follow that same pattern. I have settled for the meatloaf just so I can experience the *frosting tomorrow*. I have lived my life on the fringes, never quite having the courage or confidence to join in the fray in the middle of life. I spent my early years observing life, trying to see how it all fit together, learning the ropes, the ins and outs. Having the gifts from Spirit got me into a lot of trouble because the fear of the "unknown" perpetuated by a religious culture was used against me.

After my dad was killed, my mom sat us down one day and said, "Your dad was a good man, and God needs good men in heaven, so He took him." What I heard her say was, "If you are a good person, you will die young." I did not want to die young, so I decided to participate in life as a bad person. Of course, "bad" has many levels and definitions. I knew right from wrong and had heard and read the Ten Commandments, so my "bad" was more pranking and hurting people's feelings. These were not aspects of myself I'm proud to admit, but they were the only way I saw to keep off God's hit list for good people.

At some point, I realized that being identified as a prankster and hurtful to others was not who I really was. The only reward it was getting me was staying off God's radar. I went back to using my gifts of Spirit and stopped verbally hurting others. I did not want to be good—I just wanted to be a better person. I knew there was a fine line between good and bad, and I hugged it still. I did not have to say bad thoughts out loud; I could still think them. I became a really nice person on the outside, but walked the razor's edge of bad inside.

In 2007, I was diagnosed with stage 1 HER2 breast cancer. Harboring all those years of bad thoughts had finally caught up with me. I knew at that moment I had created my cancer. I am going to digress here a moment to share my thoughts on cancer and my own cancer story since these thoughts and my choices fly in the face of conventional medicine. Here is what I know about my cancer—this is *my* truth as *I know it* about my cancer.

From the time I felt my lump fifteen years to the day before my diagnosis, I lived in silent, hateful, and judgmental anger at my living situation at the time. The only things in my life that I did not hate were my animals and the spirits who popped in and out of my life.

Cancer is not something you catch, or something you are born with. There is no confirmed genetic cancer link between my mother, my sister, or myself, nor was there known breast cancer in my mother's mother who passed of natural causes. Cancer—my cancer—was created by my angry thoughts, plain and simple. I may have thought I was off God's radar all those years, but I was not. I am a child of the highest Spirit energy of all, good or bad. He had given me a wake-up call that got my attention 100 percent.

I had two days between my diagnosis and surgery. The White Soldier who had stood guard over me that night of my dad's death was nowhere to be seen that first night of my diagnosis. I was not angry that it happened to me. In fact, I was somewhat glad because I was so tired of walking the razor's edge. I thought about bargaining with

God, but I did not have much to bargain with. I had done some good things: served my country proudly in the U.S. Army during the Vietnam War era, had a beautiful and gifted daughter, served in the legal field as a paralegal for twenty-five years, finished my Master's degree, and taught military spouses how to be the grandest version of themselves. I advocated for children caught in the Child Protective Services system as a Court Appointed Special Advocate. This was not a lot to bargain with for fifty-seven years of living on the edge.

Even the Spirit Voices were silent that first night. I felt numb with the realization that one did not have to be good to die young; rather, being bad to escape a physical death brought on a death of one's Spirit all on its own.

I was by myself the next day as the doctor explained to me my options following surgery. Radiation and chemotherapy were explained along with the statistics of reoccurrence with each. Given my history, the fact I was still alive in my fifty-seventh year was a miracle in itself. They tell you all the good these treatment choices will do for you, but they do not mention all the side effects that could kill you just as easily, unless you ask. I had not asked.

When one is numb, one walks around in a fog, a heavy dense fog, not quite sure what to do, how to behave, or what to say. I wanted to be the one to tell my family of my diagnosis. I believed it was my story, thus my choice to tell. I thought of writing letters to those closest to me (my mother, my daughter, my horses). I think in the end, I just wrote one to my daughter. I still have it.

I am a Reiki master, but that last night I didn't even gift myself with healing. I could not—I did not—feel worthy of healing, I wanted to pay the price for my years of being bad and thinking bad thoughts. If there truly was a fair and loving God, he or she would spare my life. If not, then off to the Spirit World I would go. I was a like a sheep being led to slaughter that next morning—do this, do that, insert needle here, hook up there, just get it over. Numbness does this to you; at least it did to me. I had decided to let God make the choice—take my life or give me back a new life.

A new life comes with a price tag though. If you did not change your lifestyle, the way in which you saw your world, or your thoughts, then cancer would reoccur because nothing had changed. The only question I had to answer was whether or not I was willing to change. I knew if I lived and did not change, then the next reoccurrence would be my last.

The last image I saw before the anesthesia took effect was that of the White Soldier standing behind my surgeon. I was actually surprised to find myself alive later that night. The surgery had taken much longer than expected (the doctor laughingly thanked me for his overtime pay) and I stayed under anesthesia for way too long.

I chose to do the radiation—nineteen sessions— not the recommended thirty-six. My body was burned enough with nineteen treatments. I refused chemotherapy. The concept made no sense to me: kill everything good or bad to start again. The cancer drug I took did a number on me with aching joints, loss of energy, and lots of weight gain. I survived said drug for four years, ten months, and twenty-seven days. I was on a cruise in the middle of southeast Asia when I got up that morning and could not remember if it was pill day or not. I starred at the bottle. "I no longer need you," I said, tossing the remaining pills in the South China Sea.

I changed my lifestyle, changed who I wanted to become. I spoke my truths even though many disagreed with them. The Spirit Voices returned that day on the beach at Cape Cod. My thoughts moved from the gutter to uptown, and I concentrated on finding my own beach house. I have accepted who I am, and I am doing what I have always wanted to do—write the many stories those in the Spirit World share with me.

The path I took to get here is not the path I would recommend, unless you need the lessons it can teach along the way. You are free to learn from my lessons so your own path might be less rocky. I am not perfect; there are days I have thoughts of anger or negativity. I have learned to quickly reframe those thoughts to glass half-full words of gratitude. I am grateful for every day granted to me, for I know how quickly life can be taken away. Words of gratitude for what I do have are my anti-cancer drug of choice. To enjoy life each day is a blessing. My feet bear the scars of walking the razor's edge, and my breast the years of thinking bad thoughts. They are not scars you will ever see. You will just have to trust that they are there. When I look in the mirror, I do not see the bad person I was; I see the good person I am, warts, scars, and all.

I have been given another opportunity to do good and make a difference in the world. Let it begin with me. My cancer was my mother's meatloaf, my second chance at life the frosting leftover for tomorrow.

On this my last day and last meal, my mom's meatloaf is the best. For the first time tonight, I will not get to experience the frosting tomorrow. I will pass tonight not having the pleasure of knowing one last time that overnight can change the flavor of frosting, just as it can change the flavor of our lives, how we live them, what we achieve, and the difference we make for others.

HARVARD BEETS

I am not sure where I experienced Harvard beets for the first time, but I do remember eating them as far back as childhood, so I suspect I grew up eating them. When I went off to college, one of the easiest meals I could make on a Bunsen burner in my dorm room was Harvard beets. With a stack of saltine crackers and a can of Harvard beets, I was set for one of the many snowy evenings through those college years.

When I began working and earning my own paychecks, there were many nights that I came home from work and made Harvard beets. Saltine crackers and Harvard beets became my go-to meal when I was tired or needed to fix something quick. I thought nothing of having friends and family over and serving Harvard beets as the main course. While I could afford to buy and make different food choices, Harvard beets were a comfort food for me. I enjoyed eating them; I thought others would too.

When I joined the U.S. Army, barracks living was not too bad; mess hall eating, on the other hand, was a whole different story. I made my required appearance, had my card checked, and ate a few bites of this and that. I knew that when I got back to my room, Harvard beets and saltine crackers awaited me. Once out of basic training and out into the bigger living arena, I still found time to enjoy evenings with my Harvard beets and saltines. Once I was transferred to a tour of duty in Panama, I had to give up my Harvard beets as they were not carried in the commissary on the Atlantic side of the canal.

I could not wait to get back to the states to enjoy Harvard beets once again. A cherished care package would be one that included a few cans of sliced beets. The week I left Panama after being there three years was the week they were finally able to carry them in the commissary. Go figure.

As a single parent, money was tight and sliced beets were cheap. My daughter will not eat beets to this day, so I guess it will not be a tradition she passes on to her own children. I never did marry anyone who loved Harvard beets as much as I did, but I still continue to have them whenever I want. They make the beets in a smaller sized can now— the perfect size for my individual choice and serving. When having friends and family over for dinner, fixing my smaller sized can of Harvard beets works well. They do not have to eat them or feel guilty for not eating them. I just enjoy them one bite at a time.

In those last few hours of my life on this physical plane, I would like to savor one last time my Harvard beets and saltine crackers to remind me that no matter how much money one might have, there is always enough for Harvard beets and saltine crackers. Whatever your financial status in life, Harvard beets moves beyond the borders and infiltrates your palette with its sweet and sour taste. Life is like that you know: sweet and sour.

Jeri K. Tory Conklin

GRANDMA'S LEMON PIE

(An over 100 years-old recipe)

I remember my paternal grandmother as a stern woman, and only on a rare occasion would I see her smile. Usually those smiling moments happened when I was getting in trouble for some unknown *faux pas* I had managed to tap into. I am sure the life events she experienced growing up in the early 1900s chiseled away at her happiness. Grandma moved from Missouri to the oil fields of California as a young bride in the early 1930s. Two children soon followed: my father Doyle and my aunt Audrey. While life in the oil fields may have seemed perfect at the time, her young husband, age thirty-nine, was killed instantly on an oil rig. Grandma's life changed forever that day. A widow with two small children, she had every reason to sink to her lowest sense of herself. Instead, she turned her talents into designing flower arrangements and The Flower Shop was born. A local fixture on Main Street in Santa Paula, California, it remains today, under new owners who carry on the legacy my grandma and my father started back in those early years.

When my mom and dad married in the 1940s and had me, they all seemed to have settled into some semblance of a normal life. We never had *a lot,* but we had enough. I lived those intervening years satisfied with enough, and I was happy because I did not realize there could be more.

As I grew up and eventually moved away from home, I never forgot my grandma's lemon pie. Grandma's pie was not just *any* lemon pie; grandma's pie would melt in your mouth. Grandma would never give me her recipe, no matter how many times I begged and pleaded. She would always tell me it was a "magic recipe." I suspect that it was not that she did not want to give it to me; she just cooked with all the recipes and the measurements "a handful of this, a pinch of that" in her head. It would not be until after Grandma passed that I was able to find a written copy of her recipe.

Anxiously, I followed the written recipe to the T and, while mine was good, it was not the same as grandma's lemon pie. I played around with the recipe, tweaking it here and there. Always the same result: good, but not the melt-in-your-mouth taste that I remembered.

My friend Mia turned me onto the book *Like Water for Chocolate: A Novel in Monthly Installments with Recipes, Romance, and Home Remedies* by Laura Esquivel. Each chapter starts with a family recipe. Tita, the youngest of three daughters, is not allowed to marry, but is expected to care for her mother until her mother dies. Tita falls in love with Pedro, her soulmate. In an effort to stay close to

Tita, he marries her older sister. Having spent most of her growing up years in the kitchen cooking the traditions of her Mexican heritage, Tia learned to communicate her love and emotions through food. Angry and hurt at the injustice of not being able to marry, she bakes the wedding cake for her sister and Pedro, all the while, her tears of sorrow mixing into the batter. Sadly, everyone gets very sick.

I had never considered the concept of cooking with "love and gratitude" until I read *Like Water for Chocolate*. I began to notice that when I purposely cooked with love and gratitude, my meals tasted fresh and crisp, but mostly they tasted melt-in-your-mouth good. Perhaps the magic ingredient Grandma cooked with was *love*. As I think back all those year ago, Grandma smiled when she was cooking, all her sternness melted away. My grandparents and my family may not have had much, but just like Tita, they showed their love through the food they fed their families. Naturally, I went to my kitchen, summoned up all the love I could find within myself and I cooked Grandma's lemon pie recipe. The lemon pie of my childhood melted in my mouth once again.

This was the lesson my grandma unknowingly taught me. No matter how stern the exterior shell I wrap myself in to protect me from the harshness of life, if I hold love on the inside and cook always with love, I cannot make a bad meal. In those last few hours of my life on this physical plane, I would like to savor one last time Grandma's lemon melt-in-your-mouth pie, to remind me that the secret ingredient to experience the good in all of life's opportunities is *love*.

THIN CRACKER WAFER, HORSERADISH, AND GOLDENSEAL

Symbolizing Forgiveness for Angry Words Spoken

I had my plate planned out with the highs of my life when I realized I had no lows represented (easier to hide those). I finally allowed them to come through and while one was easily represented, I was stuck on the other. I like the symbolism of the goldenseal (bitter but healing) on top of horseradish (bitter/ angry words) on a thin wafer—similar to the host of communion, when we are reminded that all is forgiven if we just ask. The symbolism was perfect.

As a ten year-old child, I was focused on horses, and everything connected to them. My dad was a Navy pilot and had gone on one of his weekend training exercises. For some reason, he was able to come home during that week for my sister's birthday party, but had to go back the next day. I had a horse show or something that I could not go to without him, and I was not going to be able to go since he was going back. When he got ready to leave, being the ten year-old that I was, I told him I hated him and hoped he crashed. I would not even hug him good-bye. I never saw him again because he did crash the next day. There is such power in words. I knew when he crashed; I felt it. I knew when the

Navy chaplain's car showed up in the driveway what the news was going to be. In my ten-year-old mind, I believed I had been responsible for the death of my father and six others who had been killed in the crash. Families were ruined. My mother was devastated. I had no idea how much damage those few words would create.

Thirty years later, a sequence of events shed light on what really happened that day to my father and crew—the rest of the story, so to speak. I was finally able to get the accident report through the Freedom of Information Act and the truth came out. A drunk radar man had vectored his plane into the mountains on San Clemente Island. It was not the first plane he had crashed, and probably would not be the last. He was the son of a high-ranking Naval officer, and nothing was going to happen to him. It did ease my mind that my words had not caused the accident and that my father had not been piloting the plane, as I had been told in the beginning. Having said those hateful words, however, has stayed with me for the past sixty-two years, reminding me always to never say anything I will one day regret. Once out, you cannot take them back.

I needed a bitter food to remind me of those hateful words and the damage they had caused so many people. I always hoped my dad knew I really did love him; I vowed that my first question to God was going to be why He listened to the angry words of a ten-year-old child that day. This food needs to represent the hatred of the words, the guilt of killing all those people that I lived with for so many years, and at the same time, the forgiveness afforded me through grace.

A SLICE OF LEMON, SALT, AND SUGAR

My mother passed in October 2019, less than a month later than my stepsister, who passed the day after I had my stroke in September 2019.

I had called my mom that morning as I always did. She asked if I was coming to her funeral that day. I told her, "No, you are not going to die today. You still have lots of living to do."

She said, "Okay. I'm so tired."

I told her to take a nap and I would call her that afternoon.

She said, "Okay."

I said, "I love you Mom" as I hung up. She passed within a couple of hours of our phone call. I pray that she remembered the "I love you Mom" not that I would not come to her funeral that day. Little did she know, I was already there in the spirit world, watching her leave. What little connection to the Spirit World I had left allowed me to be with her as she passed.

I still pick up the phone every day to call and tell her some piece of news in my life. Like the stroke that left me missing parts of my sight, I am missing a huge piece of my heart and soul. My mother had raised us three kids after my father was killed and, to this day, I have no clue how she made it all happen. We never knew what she must have sacrificed for us. Appreciate and be grateful for everything in your life now, for one day you may find it gone without warning.

I know that I could not change the outcome of my stepsister's or my mother's journey, for these were their own birth plans and choosing. Had I not been so sick from my intestinal issues and stroke, I am sure I would have tried.

If you are wondering where the sugar fits in, somewhere, somehow, I know that my stepsister and mother are together. I know that one day, I too shall follow their journey to the light. I cannot wait to see them again when I get there, to reunite with all my soul family and most especially those heart animals that have passed before me. There is a bridge, for I have seen it in two near death experiences (NDE) of my own. Once we shed our physical bodies, there are no limits left but to experience the light like never before.

My plate is complete for now. Just as Johnny asked for foods that reminded him of those different times in his life, so too had I. In the end, it had been about the foods that reminded me of those early different and difficult times in my life where valuable lessons were learned, passed on by those who loved me most. My past has been laid to rest, and my future beckons me.

It is time to celebrate a life of memories as I walk one last time between all my choices. I cannot change the choices of my past, for they are what got me through at the time and built up change for my present and future. They are the old ways, the past, those parts of my life to leave behind. I can accept and see them in a more positive light, and so it shall be. If it is my time to go, then I am ready. I had no clue what my future held in store for me; I just prayed it was better than the past I had left behind.

Part 3

New Beginnings

Johnny Speaks to a New Beginning

Writer, all your food choices remind you's of memories in the past. What about your future? A new day? A new beginning? What about your favorite drink: your Bloody Mary? Always the same base ingredients: a spicy tomato juice, ice, vodka, but now what you's "spice/dress" it up with is always open to change. Shrimp, bacon, celery, sugar versus salted rim! Whatever you's want, add it.

Putting All the Pieces
Back Together

What is dis-ease? A condition created by the
choices and non-choices, and the consequences
of each, that one makes every day.

If it is not my time to go, then I have acknowledged
my past and I am now preparing for my future, for
new beginnings. Beginnings are bringing me back
to my soul's realignment with its purpose for this
lifetime. I allowed society to dictate who I would be
after our move to southern California, causing me
to hide who and what I really was for far too long. I
am proud of me; that is all that matters in the end.
It took four years of dis-ease to learn that lesson.
Sometimes, I guess, one has to go all the way down
the rabbit hole before one realizes the predicament
he or she is in. My rabbit hole was pretty long and I
was pretty stuck.

   If I was going to be able to survive, I needed to
find a way out without going backwards. It would

take everything I had in reserve to dig upwards and exit into a new beginning. I knew it could be done; I just had to set my intention to do so. Said intention has been set. I am ready to bring on my future.

Energy Centers and Their Roles in Our Lives

Had I been listening to my body all along, I am not sure how this current picture would look. I know all about our energy centers, or chakras, and the roles they play in our lives and our health. Why had I not remembered? I had been learning about them through all the different healing modalities I had used throughout the years. Perhaps it was time to dust them off, align, and balance them again. It was going to take strict adherence to working within my different energy centers to heal and support my body.

Our bodies are made up of energy centers. Some call these energy centers chakras. There are seven chakras. Somewhere along the way, healers began to use the term energy centers. An eighth center resides above your crown chakra and the sky. Its purpose is to connect you to your source. You the reader are free to call them whatever you are most comfortable with. I choose to use the term *energy center* and a mixture of the different definitions I have associated with same. Each energy center or chakra has its purpose and both positive and negative effects.

I was reminded of my energy centers through my Quanta-Verse and Akashic Healing class with Reese Maskwa. I began to see how the patterns in my own life had evolved. In the past, I had always found my answers on the seventh wave. I would have to return back to the sea and process the last few years to discover where I would go from there.

Our bodies were made to work in concert with our energy systems, and it does not take much to throw them all off, as mine had been. Sometime after finishing my last published book (*When Spirits Speak: A Gathering of Heroes: Stories of U.S. Soldiers in Vietnam*, 2012) and our move to southern California in 2014, I lost sight of my true self, or at least it felt that way. So many changes were happening. I had left my supportive village up in northern California and still had not found a new village that encouraged and supported me as before.

FIRST ENERGY CENTER—THE FIRST WAVE

Heal the Root, Heal the Tree

> Without a village to support and encourage
> you, you can quickly lose your sense of Self
> in an effort to be valued and accepted.

> It was in the first energy center that I began
> to see where I had initially broken down.

Upon my move to southern California and during
my series of illnesses, the Voices had gone quiet. No
one was coming through; none of my regular Voices
from the spirit world were there for me, not even
my ever-present spirit guides. Neither my spirit wolf
Akklu (my hybrid wolf in real life) nor my heart dog
Maggie (now in spirit) were to be seen. It was a very
disconcerting time.

I tried once again to find the Voices just to keep
me grounded. I took time to use my Reiki training,
and still nothing. I tried all the alternative and
holistic modalities I had learned through the years
(homeopathies, plant spirit medicine, calling on the
ancient ancestors). I was so desperate, I even called
on an extraterrestrial healer I knew of from my past
to help me—nothing. I felt so alone, as if I had been
deserted. I struggled to find my equilibrium, my
balance. I was a very small ship out on a very big

sea being tossed around in the storm, and I could not see any way out of my predicament.

It is sad to realize one is unacceptable in a new environment and community because of who the person is. For me, with my village of support gone, I found myself slowly adapting to my new surroundings. Ultimately, I became a physical desert, and my gifts from Spirit all dried up. I perceived them as dried up, gone, no longer accessible as before. Perhaps what I believe I did was instead change my focus away from them. I tucked them away in a cedar chest with many drawers. I closed the door to my cedar chest and never looked back that day.

Compassion was not my strong suit. I am sure I was last in line when it was passed out before I jumped into this lifetime. I had little, if any, compassion for others, so how could I have it for myself? I had to trust my soul would remember who I was and what I did and I was safe now. Soon I blended in with everyone else. I had become Johnny's stiltbird, who had blended in with other stiltbirds when Johnny placed it in the sand at the edge of ocean that day. I was one of "them," and I hated myself in the process. I had walked away from what I knew made me whole and happy. I heard the rooster crow and I was devastated, felt extremely isolated, left out, and alone.

I had been there for far too many years, isolated or left out. Everything culminated in my dis-ease and past four years of sickness and healing. It would be necessary to let go of relationships where I was not understood, or where my gifts were not valued. That is exactly what happened for me. I walked away from California determined to find a new village, to open up the drawers and let all my gifts out so they could once again be the light that guided my way.

Isolating experiences and relationships will lead one to become focused elsewhere in order to be valued and accepted. Being able to take a bunch of pieces of my life and put them back together so they present a complete/larger picture has taken nine years since starting this book in 2013. I stopped writing for a while after I first began Johnny's story. I was not quite ready yet to go through my pile of colorful pieces of memory.

In 2018, when I became extremely sick with intestinal issues, I saw it as just one more thing to go wrong in my life, one more avenue to isolation. However, had everything gone "wrong," as I perceived it then, or rather, had it in fact gone "right"? Maybe my soul and I had preplanned my dis-ease as a last ditch effort to find my way back should I lose sight of my divine purpose along the way.

SECOND ENERGY CENTER—THE SECOND WAVE

Riding the Wave

*Some days up, most days down, but
always rolling, never stopping*

I had felt so unsafe and disconnected from reality—
any reality. The medical field in the southern
California town we lived in had mis-diagnosed me
with Crohn's dis-ease because my gut had become
so screwed up and I had diarrhea constantly. Of
course, I had no genetic or family history of Crohn's,
but they assured me I had it. I found out later that
none of the tests run were conclusive for it. Maybe I
had it, maybe I did not.

My continued symptoms and dis-ease had not
been taken seriously. Once you have a Crohn's
diagnosis (whether correct or not) on your medical
records, there is little they will do for you except try
to control the diarrhea with drugs—many drugs—
some very toxic and destructive in fact.

My symptoms started sometime in 2018 as I
began to notice that certain foods caused different
reactions in my body. I had gone to my primary
care doctors and asked for tests to be run, but no
one took my complaint/request seriously. "People
got the runs from a variety of instances, that was
all that was going on," they said. I was not able to

change my doctors early in April 2019 when I started having more instances of loose bowels and blood. I felt like my intestines were changing/revolting and turning inside out on me. In May 2019, I started having severe pains in my intestines and two trips to the ER resulted in the medical doctor telling me, "You are just full of shit, that is the problem. Once you poop, the pain will be gone." Brilliant diagnosis doctor; I had the runs, not constipation.

In July 2019, I was back in the ER again with the same excruciating pains. The ER doc on that occasion discovered I had atrial fibrillation, (hereinafter AFib). According to the Mayo Clinic, "Atrial fibrillation is an irregular and often very rapid heart rhythm (arrhythmia) that can lead to blood clots in the heart. AFib increases the risk of stroke, heart failure, and other heart-related complications."[3] My blood pressure was through the roof due to my gut pain. The doctor gave me a small dose of morphine; the sharp pains eventually calmed down and I was sent home. He recommended I see a cardiologist to start on a medication for the AFib. Getting an appointment with a cardiologist at that time took over three months. I booked anyway for September 2019.

---

[3]   "Atrial fibrillation," Mayo Clinic, posted October 19, 2021, https://www.mayoclinic.org/diseases-conditions/atrial-fibrillation/symptoms-causes/syc-20350624.

On August 31, 2019, I had a stroke. My ER doctor that time was the same as the one in July. He asked about the AFib medicine I was to have been put on within fifteen days of leaving the hospital, or so the instructions had said. I told him I could not get an appointment until September. He immediately called his cardiologist friend and I was set up with an appointment as soon as I was released from the hospital three days later.

Losing what you never knew you had is frightening. I lost my left peripheral vision as a result of the stroke. I have taken so much of everything for granted that I really did not realize what I was missing until it was gone. How often do we do that in everyday life: not realize what we are missing until it is gone? For a month, I had visual hallucinations fill that empty spot. I never knew what would show up: slot machine wheels spinning continuously, a forest of pine trees, and later lots of colorful fall leaves filled the missing space. Even an old-fashioned oil lamp showed up one day.

I was told that they would eventually stop and there was a possibility that my vision would come back. To date, it has not. The frustrating part is not knowing what *was* before it *was not*. I did not realize until I was finishing this book that I had also lost the hearing in my left ear. I thought I was hearing just fine.

After my stroke, my symptoms of severe cramping in my intestines increased. I fired my gastroenterology specialist, and my new cardiologist recommended his friend, who got me in immediately for tests. I had CT scans, MRIs, X-rays, ultrasounds, and anything else they could think up. They all showed the same thing: an ileus, a small bowel obstruction (hereinafter SBO) at the junction of the large and small intestines. It had obviously been there since the beginning, but no one had chosen to deal with it. The Crohn's diagnosis was much easier and more profitable, it seemed. When one of my doctors let slip about the SBO having been there and seen in earlier X-rays, I started demanding action...and fast!

Despite the SBO having shown up early on, they continued to insist I had Crohn's. My own Voice became louder. I was no longer willing to spend my life in and out of the ER. Being painfully honest, I did enjoy the morphine and all the extra sleep. Upon my insistence, they began to focus on the SBO. I ended up on a thirteen-drug toxic cocktail, twice a day. They just hoped the drugs would cure whatever it was. Why not just experiment on me? That is what it felt like.

SBOs are not cured with drugs, and neither is Crohn's dis-ease. Most obstructions are cured with surgery. From August to December 2019, I was in the ER every other weekend. They called me by a new name—"Frequent Flyer"—and always had a bed waiting. Because the pain was so severe, they would start me on a morphine drip first instead of as a last resort. Trust me—it was easier that way, for them and me. Three days of morphine in the ER gave me ten days of *manageable* (and I use that word lightly) pain at home. Everyone around me recognized that neither the ER visits nor the toxic drugs were working. Only the doctors seemed blind to the fact.

On January 8, 2020, I called the ambulance to take me to ER; the pain was too unbearable. My husband saw me being loaded into the ambulance via the doorbell camera. I was rushed in with above normal gut pains. The contractions of the muscles in my back and my intestines worked together to create severe waves of pain I had no control over. I told my ER doc to just *let me die*; I could not live like this any longer. I did not have the strength or will to live one more day. Death would have been a welcomed friend. I am sure I got a double dose of morphine that night as I went to sleep very fast, not expecting to wake up in the morning. However, at 4:15 a.m. on the hospital clock dot, the blood sucker was there for a blood draw. I just laughed. There was nothing else left to do but laugh.

I am forever grateful to that ER doctor who took it upon himself to contact all the doctors on my case. By 8:00 a.m., a plan for surgery had been put in place. They had to wean me off all the toxic drugs I was on before attempting surgery. That took a good eight days—a good week with my friend Ms. Morphine in a hospital bed. You would think I would have been addicted to her by this time, but I was not. She was just the only drug that gave me release from the pain. With my AFib, I was on a blood thinner; it too had to be stopped. That was kind of scary. I did not want to have another stroke. I could not afford to lose anything else.

I was finally scheduled for a "short hour and a half" surgery on January 16, 2020. I met my surgeon, an oncologist from the cancer center near the hospital. I did not have cancer, but then I did not have leukemia either, but I had been taking a leukemia drug in hopes it would heal my SBO.

Dark Night of the Soul

I had been experiencing a very long year-and-a-half Dark Night of My Soul. My heart was in mourning for the loss of my identity, my soul. The night before my surgery was no exception. Fortunately, it seemed to culminate with this night and would decide my fate. I remember making a last ditch effort to reach out to God; perhaps He would listen, even if I was on his bad list. I bargained—begged actually—for just fifteen more years so I could outlive and bury all my dogs. It was important to me to know they had lived amazing lives and been taken care through their deaths, as I had promised them. That completed, I would be ready to go. All was quiet; not even He was answering me. At one point, I saw the White Solider standing by my side. Where He appeared in that timeline I do not know, but I was grateful He was there. If I were going to pass, I knew He would be with me, just as He had been for my Dad and soldiers everywhere.

I remember nothing of that next day: what happened before the surgery, when they came to get me, being wheeled down the hall to the surgery room—nothing. When I told my surgeon that I did not remember anything a few weeks later at one of my check-ups, he said, "Be thankful that you don't remember anything about that day. And I pray you never will."

I am unaware of when I came out of surgery, what time it might have been, whether it was that night or the next day. I do remember waking up in the dark, hearing a small Voice coming through the ethers of my mind. I could not move, I did not want to move. I was surprised I was still alive, though I was not sure why. What did I have left to live for?

The Voice called again, "Writer, are you there?"

I answered the Voice, "I'm here. Who are you?"

"Writer, I'm Soldier Blue," he said. "I want you to write my story." I could hear the merriment of the children's voices I was familiar with in the background. They had been gone for the past few years and I had missed them. Shaking the anesthesia-induced sleep and cobwebs from my head, I asked what his story was about.

"I'm a Union soldier. I was killed in the war."

I saw Soldier Blue sitting on a large boulder in a river with a rudimentary fishing pole, dressed in a ragged, blood-stained uniform. "The Shenandoah River," he said, without my asking.

My next book was waiting for me. "Sure," I told him, "but I have to heal first." He just smiled as the river ran past him. I knew I was going to be okay. The Universe was not done with me yet; I still had a purpose to fulfill. I said, "Thank you" to God, just in case He was listening this time. My Dark Night of the Soul was finally over. For the first time, in a very long time, I was at peace.

I was told later that my surgery had required six and one-half long hours. Because my SBO had been ignored for so long and because of the damage done by the toxic drug cocktail I was on, my surgeon had to remove 18 inches of dead, ulcerated bowel, as well as the SBO. My surgeon was quite surprised I had been able to live with it as long as I had.

I spent twenty-six days in the hospital, going through the motions of healing. I had so many things I needed to learn about physical management of my incision and movement behaviors.

I will not kid you: healing from the surgery I had was not easy—not at all *a walk in the park,* as some say it is. There were days I wished I was dead. One of the nurses who came every day to take vitals and so on told me it would take me at least a year to start feeling "normal," whatever my new "normal" would be. I laughed at her. She had to be kidding. She was not. In fact, it is now going on two years and I am just now, having met my new holistic healing village, beginning to finally heal.

THIRD ENERGY CENTER—THE THIRD WAVE

When survival mode kicks in, listen.

Two months into my healing process, while still in California, I felt my fight or flight survival mechanism kick in. It would not let me rest. I knew I had to leave the state as soon as possible. I have felt the survival mode kick in before while in the military, but never as strong as it felt this time. I had to listen—I had to.

COVID-19 restrictions had been instituted and virtually locked California down. Still, we drove down to Arizona anyway; my sister and brother-in-law had bought property there and were building a house. After two days of exhaustive looking at house after house, we bought our place here in Prescott Valley. I could not move in quickly enough.

FOURTH ENERGY CENTER—THE FOURTH WAVE

Natural healers bring us back into wholeness through love and self-acceptance.

Remember when I had my stroke and said, "You don't know what you have until you lose it"? Well, I was so concentrated on healing and finding a new normal, as the old one was long gone, that I did not realize I did not remember the simple things. I did not remember how to cook. I would stare at the food, waiting for it to do something; when it did not, I would walk away. I did not remember how to clean a house, how to wash and iron clothes. I used to design and make beautiful Reiki pillows to sell, but I did not even remember how to sew the materials together. I just stared at the sewing machine, not knowing how to thread it—nothing. People take for granted so many things. I did not realize how much I had actually forgotten until this year. I wanted to be *normal* again, but I no longer knew what *normal* was going to look like. Learning to live with a new *normal* is not, and was not, easy. I would abdicate my life decisions to someone else during this time.

It was easier just to hide the fact I did not remember something than to say, "I don't remember how to..." and feel like a failure. Even though I had gotten the call from Soldier Blue to write his story, I did not walk out of the hospital, pick up a pen, and start writing. First, I would finish this book. Soldier Blue's book would have to wait—and waiting patiently he is, fishing from his favorite rock in the middle of the Shenandoah River. It would take me another year to begin writing again. The words were swimming in my head; getting them down on paper was not guaranteed. It would not be until I met Catherine Marie at The Grateful Heart in Prescott, Arizona, who told me to "go write the words," that I was able to come home, pull out this story, and finish writing.

Sometimes all you need is encouragement, someone who never doubts your ability telling you "you can." There are people on the outskirts of your village—"outliers," I call them. They might not be able to be a part of your village for whatever reason, but they know your worth. They see your potential and will keep gently urging you to action. Listen to them; do not turn away. They see in you something you may not see in yourself. Be grateful for their persistence. They see behind the curtain hiding the wizard inside you. They know you better than you know yourself, and they remember who *you* are.

One thing about moving to Arizona is that the holistic medicine profession and community are amazing here. I found a holistic practitioner named Jane. Jane recognized my soul the minute I walked in. She knew who I was inside the mask I wore for the public and what was happening to my body from a nutrition standpoint. It was so good to be able to talk with someone about my communication with the Spirit World, being a Reiki Master, and the energy healing I once did. I walked out of her office feeling free, as if I had been rescued and able to be me for the first time in a couple of years. I also left with a sack full of remedies, some affirmations, and the feeling I had found a special friend, a new villager. My physical body needed her nutritional suggestions to begin to balance itself.

Not long after, I was able to find someone able to do energy work on my emotional, physical, and mental body systems. I made an appointment with him for the next week. My work was not easy, and we worked through many layers of what I called my "missing years." We were able to unblock so many of the energy blocks that occurred as a result of my becoming a desert and moving my focus away from the Spirit World while in southern California.

Sometimes you just need to find a healer who brings you back to yourself through love and acceptance of yourself.

FIFTH ENERGY CENTER—THE FIFTH WAVE

For the second time, I was feeling that small spring of excitement bubbling up inside of me. Perhaps now I had the beginnings of a healing village to encourage and support me, and I could be me again: the Writer who the children, the soldiers, now Johnny and the others, came to for their stories to be told. I was ready and waiting for that long dry spell to be over, to once again feel the energy and excitement of working with the Spirit World.

I learned it is never too late to get off your chosen path and find your way back on your true path. That is exactly what I did when I found my new village here in Arizona and Costa Rica. They all helped me in different ways to find my way back to who my soul longed to be.

I pulled out each of my published books and began reading their introductions again. It was that "remembering back" that brought me back to life. I was once again the student the Universe had mentored all those years ago. I remembered who I was: a child of the Universe, writing for the Spirit World, born in the stars which I have always called home. I had been, and was, good at it. And then there was Soldier Blue, waiting quietly on a boulder in the middle of the Shenandoah River for me to be ready to write his story.

SIXTH ENERGY CENTER—THE SIXTH WAVE

Still, it would take Catherine Marie to push me farther into my being. She laid out the cards from the Medicine Card deck (my favorite and well-used deck) and Raven, my spirit animal, appeared in the spread. Whatever mental/emotional dams I had been holding back burst as Raven came forth to give me my Voice back to speak my truths. Catherine is an intuitive and said my words would comfort and heal many. I was excited about that. I loved writing; the words just seemed to flow, and it was time I could spend with those who had passed. Catherine energetically knitted and purled some of my energy fields back together that day and worked on me for the next few days as the layers of dust disappeared from my energy field. I felt as if I glowed once again and whatever lingering doubts I had of who I was were gone. I knew I had another villager and friend, a part of my soul group actually. My inner child, the one that had been silenced long ago, asked if Catherine Marie knew her. Catherine smiled, and said she did. That is the amazing way soul groups work. I had found her when the time was right and not before. Long ago, before coming into this lifetime, we had agreed to meet so she could help me.

SEVENTH ENERGY CENTER/EIGHTH ENERGY CENTER—THE SEVENTH WAVE

I know I said in my introduction that my answers always came on the seventh wave. I have combined both the seventh and eighth energy centers as they both contained the answers for my seventh wave. Not long after meeting Catherine Marie, I had picked up where I had left off in this book and started writing on Johnny's story. While I was hearing the Voices again and talking with the spirits, I knew I was still missing something—but what? Would it be my purpose for coming into this lifetime and the lessons I had to learn?

No one needs to do what I did—develop a disease to bring me back to who I am. Sit quietly and "remember back." That still, small Voice inside of you will show you your way back to who you are and what you were meant to do in this lifetime. The southern California medical community was not my friend, though I am grateful to the surgeon who saved my life. Find a community that works with you through the alternative healing modalities available to us all. Our bodies know how to heal themselves if we give them the right energies and nourishment. Our ancient ancestors did not have corner pharmacies to run to. They just used that which God had provided them through the healing energies and plants, passing said knowledge down through their oral histories. There are no limitations except for those you create for your own benefit.

Changing the Channel

If you do not like the channel you are watching, change it until you find the one that fits. I happened upon a website link posted on Facebook by a person named Reese Maskwa, a Trauma and Spiritual Transformational Expert, who I have spoken about earlier. She was advertising Akashic Soul Blueprint Reports[4]. After getting it arranged on Costa Rican time, she sent me my report. It blew me away. It did not say anything that wasn't 100 percent true. Reese was the real deal. We emailed back and forth with some questions and answers and I knew she would be the next addition to my village. A few weeks later, she told me of a class she was teaching on Quanta-Verse and Akashic Healing. The universe had sent all these people to me. I was not ready to stop now. I was finally on the best channel for my growth.

I am currently taking her Quanta-Verse and Akashic Healing class, and I cannot tell you the change it has made in me, and I have made in

---

4   For more information, visit www.quanta-verse.com.

myself. It is as if I am finally grounded and back on my path of what I came into this lifetime to do and learn. I am strong enough now, with the help of my Arizona and Costa Rican village, to stand up for what I believe in. I believe in myself, my gift of communication, my gifts of healing, and purpose in this lifetime. The seventh wave had not disappointed with its answers. Wisdom, ancient wisdom, endures through the ages. It will never lead you astray. Trust it, listen to it. It will guide you always.

Afterword
A Message of My Own (2022)

*Our tragedies and pain bring us to
where we need to be to heal others.*
Reese Maskwa

Nothing ever has to stay the same. Let creativity flow into all you touch, speak, write. Even your plating of this last/first meal may speak to your creativity. Every thought you think is a creation of its own. I accept full responsibility for creating my dis-ease and everything surrounding it. Do I wish I had done it differently? Perhaps. I guess I needed the lessons this particular path afforded me. Never forget that every one of you came into this lifetime to create. Do it! When you stumble across a quotation or something that catches your attention, grab onto it, claim it, and make it yours.

Joe Haourton Hanrath did a collective card pull today (June 4, 2022) using *the Gateway of Light*

Activation Oracle: A 44-card Deck and Guidebook by Kyle Gray. It spoke to me and I claimed it. It said

> **Whenever the Akashic Stargate is presented to you, it's because you're at a critical point on your journey. You have the opportunity to move in a particular direction and you have to make a decision. This can feel overwhelming and you may be waiting for someone or something to make the decision for you. But you aren't here to walk a path that was set for you, you're here to walk a path that you have chosen. The next phase of your journey cannot unfold until you decide which way to go. Know that whatever direction you take and whatever decision you make, you'll always be on the right path. No matter how you get there, you'll always end up in a similar space. Also know that purpose isn't about doing your duty, it's about living life and experiencing joy.[5]**

I am back, I am there, this book is finished, and I am no longer invisible like the stiltbird among those who walk this earth and inhabit the sky. I am proud of who I am and who I am becoming. I look forward to finishing learning the lessons I came into this lifetime to learn, to helping others make a difference and find themselves.

---

[5] Joe Haourton Hanrath, Facebook post, June 4, 2022.

I now have a full beach house (my inner center) of spirit guides who have been with me for quite a while. I cannot wait to begin working with each of them again. So many new ideas were suggested today as I met with them. I have many books to write in my future, languages to download and explore to bring forth some truths and wisdoms that have long been silenced.

Having conversations with Winterhawk, one of my spirit guides and a husband in my past Native American life, is the "frosting" I was missing from mom's meatloaf. I realized I could have it in my future; it wasn't only for my past. In fact, I am experiencing all the foods of my past today, in my current life, though I am seeing them through a different set of lenses.

This journey into finding and hearing my Voice has been healthy. The words were just waiting for an invitation to spring forth. I have much to say through my words, to honor all we are, and to bring hope that there is a world, another life, after this one—a new beginning.

Johnny was correct. A Bloody Mary is the perfect representation of my future, because what I want to add to it has no limits. I traveled back to California last year (2021) with my sister for my niece's wedding. We stopped in Tehachapi for dinner and I had their featured Bloody Mary. It had at least fifteen different additions. All I can remember is a Zing Zang® Bloody Mary base with vodka and fried chicken on a stick, bacon-wrapped shrimp, asparagus spears, celery, olives, pearl onions, a dill pickle spear, a cheeseburger slider, a bacon-wrapped pepper, a scallop, a boiled egg, and a few other things I cannot remember. I do remember the glass it came in was *huge*. I believe I somehow managed to eat/drink most of it.

As I think back on that day, perhaps it was a turning point for me to realize that the world was open to me. I was free to do and be anything I wanted. I could fill my life with any variety of ingredients each day. So can you if you make that choice.

I learned in finding my own Voice that what you put into living, you get back. But *you* have to put it in; daydream and visualize whatever/however you want your life to be. Just like my mom knew it was her day to pass from this lifetime into her next, let today become the first day of your new life! Here's to Bloody Mary drinks everywhere!

What does my future hold? In that next chapter in my life, words—lots and lots of words—will flow from my mouth, words born deep in my soul, just waiting for an opportunity to come forth. These words will guide others into their own futures. These words will bring forth the truth for all to hear, as we gather as *one* to move forward into new beginnings. These words are meant to bring healing to many a searching soul. These are words to weave ourselves back together when our energy is fractured by everyday life within this society. "Words to speak our futures," says the Raven.

Remember the magic always!

Recipes

From "Stiltbird's Last Supper"

Fried Corn

1/4 cup bacon drippings
10 ears fresh corn, cleaned, kernels cut from cob
1/4 cup milk
1 teaspoon salt
1/2 teaspoon pepper

In an iron skillet, heat drippings over medium heat. Add corn and cook about 5 minutes, then add milk, salt, and pepper. Remove from stove and serve.

Fried Green Tomatoes

(Grandmammy's recipe)
Green Tomatoes
Eggs and Milk
Flour or cornmeal

Grandmammy just sliced them tomatoes, sprinkled with salt and pepper, dipped them in her egg and milk (or sometimes water when we didn't have milk) mixture; then dipped in either flour or cornmeal (again, depended on what we's had at the time). Fry them in really hot oil in a hot skillet and then drain on a rack. They's just melted in your mouth.

Johnny's Tin Can Cornbread

I have no recipe, Writer. I just mixed up some cornmeal when I could with some water in a washed out tin can I's found along the road. I would cook it over my evening fire. It wasn't nice and fluffy like Grandmammy's cornbread, but it would fill the hole in my tummy.

———⁂———

From "Frequency Interrupted"

Milk Coffee with My Dad

1/2 coffee cup of fresh perked coffee
1/2 cup of milk (fresh from the cow is the best)
A heaping spoonful of sugar

Mom's Meatloaf

Heat oven to 350 degrees. Cooking
time is approximately 1 hour.

Mix the following ingredients together
and put in loaf pan (bread pan) or
shape like a loaf in square pan.

1 1/2 pounds ground hamburger
(I normally use 2 pounds)
2/3 cup breadcrumbs
1 cup milk
1 egg
1/4 grated onion or 1/4 cup dry chopped onion
1 teaspoon salt
1/2 teaspoon sage
Pepper to taste

Frosting

Combine 3 tablespoons brown sugar, 1/4 cup catsup, 1/4 teaspoon nutmeg and 1 teaspoon dry mustard. Spread on top of meatloaf and bake. (Because I love the frosting most, I double the recipe so I know there is plenty of frosting for the next day's sandwiches.)

Harvard Beets

1 can sliced beets, including 1/2 of the juice
1/4 cup sugar
1/4 cup apple cider vinegar
Mix and heat on the stove. Once it starts to boil, add a mixture of 1 tablespoon cornstarch with 1/4 cup of water, or whatever mixture you prefer to use for the purpose of thickening the beet juice. Don't walk away as it thickens very quickly.

Grandma's Lemon Pie

(An over 100 years-old recipe)

1 1/2 cups sugar
1/3 cup corn starch
1 1/2 cup hot water
Mix together first three ingredients on the stove.

Add 3 egg yolks, slightly beaten.
Add some of the above mixture to
yolks first to "temper" them.

Add to the above mixture
3 tablespoons of butter
1/4 cup lemon juice (fresh squeezed is best)
1/3 cup grated lemon rind
Cook in a double broiler until thick. (I use a
regular sauce pan and really watch the heat),
stirring constantly. Once it is of a "pudding"
consistency, pour into a baked pie shell.

Cover with peaks of whipped egg white meringue.

Meringue

3 egg whites
1/4 teaspoon salt
6 tablespoons sugar

Bake at 400 degrees approximately 10 minutes,
or just until the peaks of meringue are brown.

ACKNOWLEDGMENTS

Someone once said, "It takes a village to raise a child." I believe it also takes a village to bring a book to fruition. Once I started acknowledging those who had made a difference in my own journey with this book and my new beginning, I realized I was blessed to have quite a few beautiful souls in my village.

To the spirit children and soldiers who have passed, the greatest *thank you* as you brought forth Johnny and myself for this adventure.

To Teri Ann "Sunny" Henderson (my own beautiful, talented, and gifted daughter), thank you for the beautiful illustration of the Stiltbird that graces the cover of this book.

To my husband, Kurt, thank you for your belief in my ability to write and publish this book. Your eyes and the way you've expertly smoothed over the transitions have been invaluable. Thank you also for picking up the slack when I was so sick. It was easier to let you do it than see myself as a failure.

To Chris Addington, thank you for the amazing logo. The spirit children inspired it, and you brought it out in your beautiful pen and ink drawing. The children approve it!

To Linda Ouellette, who encourages me daily not to give up when the going gets hectic and challenging, and who is always there for me with her words of strength and love. Little did either of us know how important a role she would play in my healing journey.

To Suzanne Marlow, a long-time friend brought together by our love for our Brittanys, you had faith in me when I had lost mine. Thank you.

To Reese Maskwa, my Costa Rican connection, who opened my soul to healing and reminded me of my purpose for this lifetime, and for sticking with me through the weeks of Quanta–Verse and Akashic Healing classes. The classes she teaches showed me the way back to who I was born to be, so I could use the gifts I was born with for the benefit of all.

To Catherine Marie of The Grateful Heart, who spoke those words I needed to hear at the time I was ready to give up my spiritual gifts.

To Jane, for guiding me to balance my body energies after all the damage had been done. Your insight is amazing, and my body and I are most grateful.

To Steven, for all the layers you removed to help me heal. You are an extremely gifted, *Energy Systems Connector extraordinaire.*

To Reita Robertson, who approached me with a problem requiring communication with a disenchanted spirit from her past life, and trusted me with the outcome. Reita has begun her own journey into the gifts of healing. What is that saying, "When the teacher is ready, the student will come"? Thank you Reita. You will never know how much I appreciate and need you to get me started again. I am honored to be one of your teachers in my own small way.

To my brother Stan and sister Candy—we are all that is left. We are bonded together by more than just a family name. When this life is over, we have another amazing one waiting. Looking forward to seeing you both on the other side. You are the best, and I am so happy to be a part of us now.

To Solider Blue, the Voice that brought me back from the edge of the precipice, patiently waiting for his turn to speak.

To all those who assisted in the publication process of this book, my editors, my Balboa Press design team, and friends who helped further my research, your assistance was invaluable.

To anyone along this journey who I have forgotten to mention, thank you for the lessons along the way and for being part of my village. You have all been important teachers in this lifetime. Some of you I am sure I will see as major players in the next one.

And to the sea, my forever friend, thank you as always, for my answers on the seventh wave.

BIBLIOGRAPHY

"Atrial fibrillation." Mayo Clinic. Posted October 19, 2021. https://www.mayoclinic.org/diseases-conditions/atrial-fibrillation/symptoms-causes/syc-20350624.

Haourton Hanrath, Joe. Facebook post. June 4, 2022.

Madison, Nicole. "What are the Restriction[s] on Last Meal[s]?" My Law Questions. Last modified June 26, 2022. https://www.mylawquestions.com/what-are-the-restrictions-placed-on-a-last-meal.htm.

Printed in the United States
by Baker & Taylor Publisher Services